Not a Bean

Click,

clack!

Claudia Guadalupe
Martínez

Illustrated by
Laura González

ini Charlesbridge

Next to the arroyo
a seedpod grows
on the yerba de la flecha,
a desert shrub.

The seedpod is
made of smaller pods,
each a bean
that is **Not a Bean.**

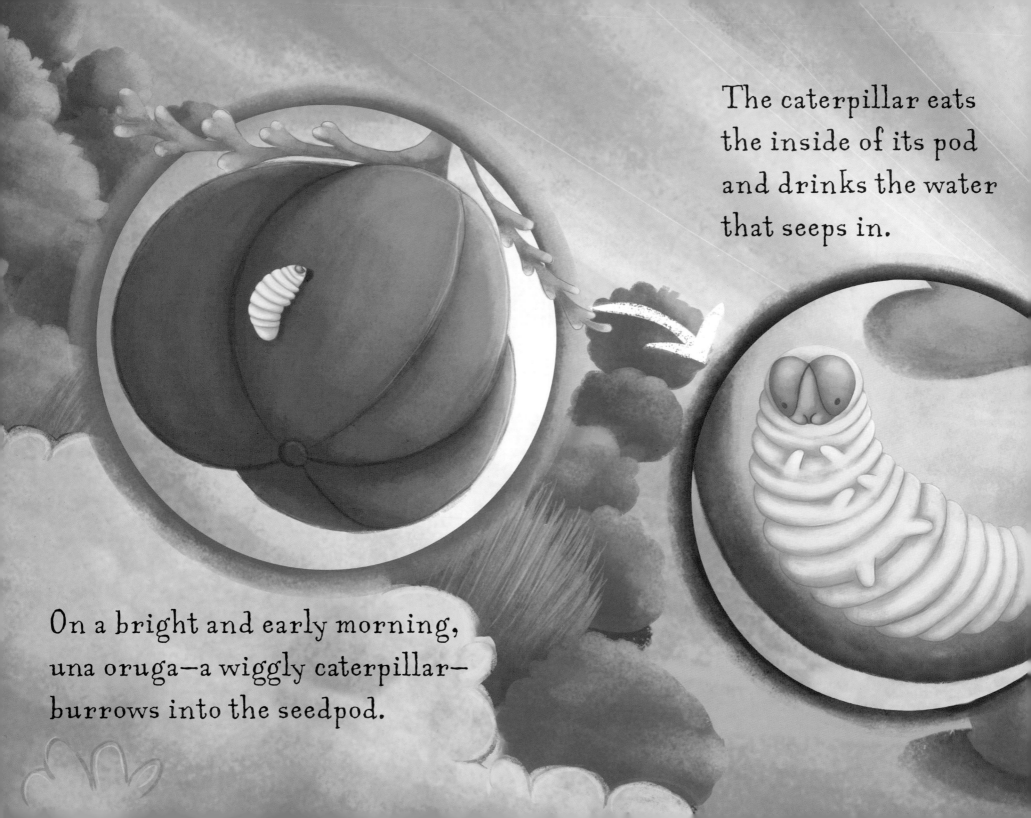

The caterpillar eats the inside of its pod and drinks the water that seeps in.

On a bright and early morning, una oruga—a wiggly caterpillar—burrows into the seedpod.

Later, the seedpod
dries and hardens.
It splits and falls
to the ground.

Click,

clack!

Midmorning, dos saguaros
hold prickly arms up high
as el sol scorches
everything in sight.

The caterpillar inside the **Not a Bean** rolls it into the shade.

Click,

clack!

At noon, tres cascabeles slither from their nests among the rocks. Their tails rattle.

The **Not a Bean** jumps to safety and lands inside a crack.

Click, clack!

Early afternoon,
cuatro coyotes scope the land.
They sniff the wind.
They howl.

The **Not a Bean** jumps.
The coyotes
startle and run!

Click, clack!

Midafternoon, cinco cuervos escape a storm and perch near the pod. They chatter. The **Not a Bean** jumps. The cuervos scatter.

Click, clack!

Late afternoon, seis nubes
send rain down hard and fast.
The arroyo fills and floods.

The **Not a Bean** rocks.
It rides the waves.

Click, clack!

Siete amigos explore.
They look for treasures
washed up by the rain.

The friends scoop up
the jumping bean that is
Not a Bean.

Click, clack!

That evening, the amigos
draw ocho óvalos for
a game in the dirt.
The friends clap.

The **Not a Bean** jumps.
They place it in the center,
along with others.

Click, clack!

Nueve saltarines hold
still in the silence.
The amigos cheer for
their jumping beans.

Click,

clack!

The jumping beans roll
into the ovals.
"¡Bravo! ¡Bravo!"

At night, diez estrellas
twinkle in the sky.
"Buenas noches,"
someone says.

Click,

clack!

The **Not a Bean** jumps.
But then it's quiet again.

The amigos return.
They sing and clap.
They poke the **Not a Bean**
with a stick, but it doesn't jump.

So go many days under
the desert cielo.
The caterpillar inside
the **Not a Bean** is busy
spinning a cocoon.

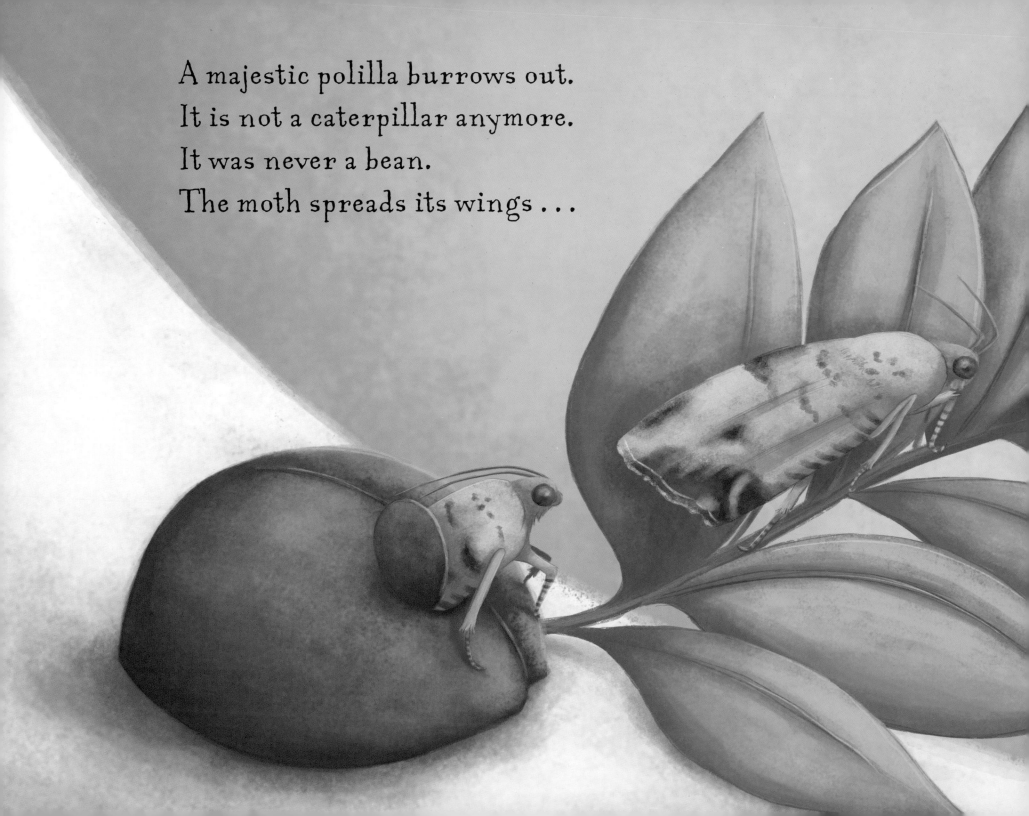

A majestic polilla burrows out.
It is not a caterpillar anymore.
It was never a bean.
The moth spreads its wings . . .

...and soars into the sky.

GLOSSARY

AMIGOS: friends

ARROYO: stream

BUENAS NOCHES: good night

CASCABELES: rattlesnakes

CIELO: sky

COYOTES: small relatives of the gray wolf

CUERVOS: crows

ESTRELLAS: stars

NUBES: clouds

ORUGA: caterpillar

ÓVALOS: ovals

POLILLA: moth

SAGUAROS: tree-like cacti

SALTARINES: jumpers

SOL: sun

YERBA DE LA FLECHA: (literally "herb of the arrow") a type of flowering shrub

COUNT TO TEN

UNA/UNO: one

DOS: two

TRES: three

CUATRO: four

CINCO: five

SEIS: six

SIETE: seven

OCHO: eight

NUEVE: nine

DIEZ: ten

Click, clack!

AUTHOR'S NOTE

Yerba de la flecha (scientific name *Sebastiana pavoniana*) is a shrub that grows along arroyos in the northern desert mountains of Mexico. Its leathery leaves are dark green and turn red as the seasons change. The stems exude a poisonous milky sap, which is said to have been used to poison the tips of arrows—hence the plant's name (herb of the arrow).

Female jumping bean moths (scientific name *Laspeyresia saltitans*) lay their eggs on the yerba de la flecha's seedpods. Once the eggs hatch, the baby caterpillars (larvae) eat their way inside the seedpods. Eventually the seedpods mature, break off, and split into pieces. Any piece that has a larva inside is a so-called jumping bean.

The pods provide both shelter and food for the larvae. The larvae survive by drinking moisture that collects inside the pods when it rains and by jumping to escape the heat. Vibrations of sound or movement also cause them to jump, warding off predators such as birds and small mammals.

As time goes by, the caterpillars enter the pupal stage and spin a cocoon inside the pod, where they undergo metamorphosis and transform into moths.

They emerge as gray or silver-colored adult moths. The females fly off into the desert and lay their eggs, repeating the life cycle.

Outside their desert home, jumping beans can be found in novelty shops. In a popular game, children make playing boards like the one shown in this book, drawing a circle with numbered ovals surrounding it. The children choose a number from one to four and place jumping beans in the middle, getting the pods to move by cheering, singing, or turning on the radio. When the first bean enters a numbered oval, the child with that number wins. In another version of the game, children choose a bean and place it in the middle of the circle. The child whose bean crosses first into any of the ovals is the winner.

While as many as twenty million jumping beans have been harvested in a year, most yearly numbers are much smaller. The moths need the yerba de la flecha to lay their eggs, and if environmental changes affect the plant, the moths can't reproduce.

I learned about jumping beans when I was a little girl. I purchased three from the local discount store and studied them with my older brother. We didn't know then how far from home the jumping beans had come. Now I like to imagine the moths they became, flying off into the sunset, free.

Text copyright © 2019 by Claudia Guadalupe Martínez
Illustrations copyright © 2019 by Laura González

Published by Charlesbridge
85 Main Street
Watertown, MA 02472
(617) 926-0329
www.charlesbridge.com

Library of Congress Cataloging-in-Publication Data
Names: Martínez, Claudia Guadalupe, 1978– author. | González, Laura, illustrator.
Title: Not a bean / Claudia Guadalupe Martínez ; illustrated by Laura González.
Description: Watertown, MA : Charlesbridge, 2019.
Identifiers: LCCN 2017035916 (print) | LCCN 2017047984 (ebook) |
ISBN 9781632896674 (ebook) | ISBN 9781632896681 (ebook pdf) |
ISBN 9781580898157 (reinforced for library use)
Subjects: LCSH: Moths—Juvenile literature. | CYAC: Jumping bean—Juvenile literature.
Classification: LCC QL544.2 (ebook) | LCC QL544.2 .M2582 2019 (print) | DDC
595.78—dc23
LC record available at https://lccn.loc.gov/2017035916

Printed in China
(hc) 10 9 8 7 6 5 4 3 2 1

Illustrations created in Photoshop
Hand-lettering of title by Laura González
Text type set in Aunt Mildred by MVB Design
Color separations by Colourscan Print Co Pte Ltd, Singapore
Printed by 1010 Printing International Limited in Huizhou, Guangdong, China
Production supervision by Brian G. Walker
Designed by Joyce White & Jacqueline Cote

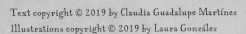

FOR MY THREE AMIGOS: PENNY,
TOBY, AND HARLEY— C. G. M.

TO EMMA VICTORIA— L. G.

*Caterpillar, seedpod, and moth
on this page are actual size.